FAIRY RINGS and OTHER MUSHROOMS

FAIRY RINGS and

GLADYS CONKLIN

OTHER MUSHROOMS

Illustrated by Howard Berelson

Holiday House · New York

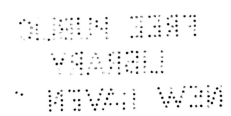
LIBRARY OF CONGRESS CATALOGING IN PUBLICATION DATA

Conklin, Gladys (Plemon)
Fairy rings and other mushrooms.

SUMMARY: Introduces the characteristics of a variety
of mushrooms and some of the folklore connected with them.
1. Mushrooms—Juvenile literature. [1. Mushrooms]
I. Berelson, Howard, 1943-   illus. II. Title.
QK603.5.C66   589'.222   73-76799
ISBN 0-8234-0223-1

For Irving and Teen . . .
two mushroom enthusiasts

Introduction

People have been puzzled about mushrooms for hundreds of years. Many legends and folk tales have developed about these curious plants.

Mushrooms are a part of the group of plants called fungi (pronounced *funj*-eye; singular, *fun*-gus). They cannot make their own food, as other plants do. They usually grow where it is wet and damp. Each type of mushroom does best in a particular area. Some grow on dead or rotting wood; others grow on live trees. Some grow in dirt or moss. They are as colorful and beautiful as wild flowers. They come in colors of red, yellow, purple, green, orange, and brown.

Mushrooms are plants without leaves. The mushroom that you see is the fruit of the plant. The plant itself grows underground. Like all fruit, the mushroom produces a kind of seeds that are called spores. Unlike most seeds, they carry almost no food to start growing with. These spores are so small that they can be seen only under a powerful microscope.

There are different ways of producing spores. In two common types of mushroom, the spores are produced in gills—a set of thin plates—and in tubes. Both types develop spores on the underside of the mushroom cap. When the mushroom is ripe, the spores fall. Some may drop directly to the ground but most of them are scattered by the wind. Most of the mushrooms die when all the spores have fallen.

The spores may be white, pink, yellow, brown, or black. The color is important in helping the scientist to identify the species. When a spore sprouts, it grows into a thick white mass of threads called a mycelium. This is the plant of the mushroom.

Many mushrooms are excellent to eat. They may taste like fried chicken, oysters, cauliflower, or even steak. Often an edible mushroom—one you can safely eat—and a poisonous one look almost alike. Some poisonous mushrooms will make you very ill and a few can cause death. WILD MUSHROOMS SHOULD BE PICKED FOR EATING ONLY BY EXPERTS WHO CAN IDENTIFY THE POISONOUS KINDS. The rest of us should be content to enjoy the beauty of the wild mushroom in its woodsy setting.

There is no way to tell if a mushroom is poisonous except to know and recognize the parts of it. The poisonous mushrooms are eaten by wild creatures with no bad results. Deer nibble on them; snails and salamanders eat them; squirrels carry them off to their nests to enjoy them. But you and I dare not swallow one bit of a poisonous mushroom.

The difference between a mushroom and a toadstool has confused people for many years. Dr. Daniel E. Stuntz, a professor of botany at the University of Washington, says there is no difference; they are the same plant. He explains that the word "toadstool" has long carried with it the idea of poison—apparently because centuries ago, toads were thought to be poisonous and people had the notion that they sat on mushrooms and transferred poison to them in this way.

There are many very tiny mushrooms growing in moss and on old logs. To enjoy the sight of these, you should carry a hand lens (a magnifying glass) with you. A hand lens will take you into a fantastic world that your eyes alone will miss.

The species—or exact kinds—of mushrooms in this book are the common ones found throughout the United States. Some of them are found all over the world. Since their common names vary, and often cover many different kinds of mushrooms (and even other plants), species names are the best ones to go by. This book is to help you discover some of the beauty and color and wonder of the mushroom family.

For further reading:

Mushrooms and Molds, by Robert Froman (Thomas Y. Crowell, 1972)

Plants Without Leaves, by Ross E. Hutchins (Dodd, Mead, 1966)

The Story of Mosses, Ferns, and Mushrooms, by Dorothy Sterling (Doubleday, 1955)

The Wonders of Fungi, by Lucy Kavaler (John Day, 1964)

Gladys Conklin

Species names are given in italic type.

Bird's Nest   *Crucibulum laeve*

This little fungus resembles a bird's nest. It is so small that you need a hand lens to enjoy its tiny beauty. The nests are about the size of your little fingernail. They grow on small sticks and twigs on the ground and there are usually many of them close together. You may walk over them a dozen times before you discover the smallness of them.

The nest is covered while it is growing. This protects the spores that are developing inside in the "eggs." When the spores are ripe, the cover splits open and you will see a white nest about half full of tiny light-brown eggs. The eggs contain the spore of the fungus. When they are hit by raindrops, the eggs pop out of the nest and the spores are scattered by the wind.

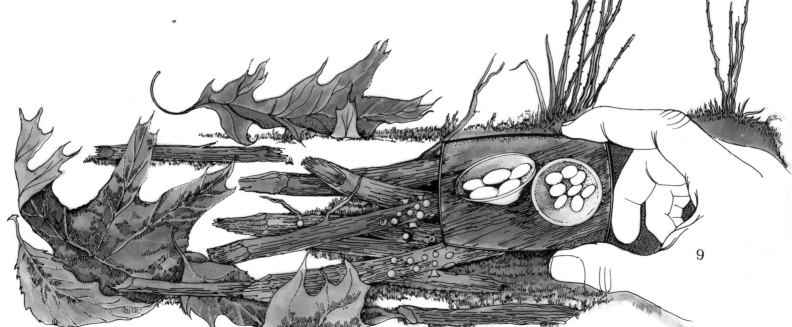

9

Cauliflower Mushroom *Sparassis radicata*

A cauliflower mushroom is a surprising plant to find growing in the woods. It is white with a light splash of yellow all over. It is good to eat when it is young and grows to be one of the largest of our edible mushrooms. Some are about the size of our garden cauliflower but it isn't unusual to find one that weighs from 40 to 50 pounds. It grows in evergreen forests at the base of a tree. It is a parasite on trees and may appear year after year on the same tree. It is considered a prize by the experts who gather mushrooms. Look for it from July to October.

Golden Chanterelle   *Cantharellus cibarius*

When you discover this mushroom, you have a feeling that it is like finding a pot of gold at the foot of a rainbow. It is a golden yellow from the top of the cap to the bottom of the stem. It grows in clusters from June to October in most wooded areas in the United States. It is usually on mossy ground or on dead leaves, and it often grows in circles. It is good to eat, but more than that, it is beautiful to look at. If you are walking under pine trees, watch for a golden shimmer that may be just ahead of you, especially after a hard rain.

11

Chicken-of-the-Woods   *Polyporus sulphureus*

When cooked in butter, this mushroom tastes like crisp fried chicken. It is strikingly beautiful as you look at it high up on the side of a tree. It grows in large wavy caps, one on top of another, like painted shelves. The caps are brilliantly colored a bright orange on top with sulphur-yellow underneath. They are large, as much as 20 inches wide. Look for them during wet weather from May to October.

You may see woodpeckers in the area where you find this colorful mushroom. They help to scatter the spores. If you see a woodpecker land on a tree, notice how he uses his tail for a prop. His tail feathers may rub against the mushroom and pick up spores. When he flies off to another tree, he rubs the spores off in a new place and a fresh cluster of mushrooms is started.

12

Destroying Angel *Amanita virosa*

This mushroom is called the destroying angel partly because it is a beautiful shimmering white and partly because it is deadly poisonous. Too many careless people pick it and die from eating it. There are other white mushrooms in the woods that are not poisonous, but it takes an expert to tell them apart. It is safest not to touch any of the all-white mushrooms. Enjoy their delicate beauty and leave them as they are for the pleasure of others who want to see them.

13

Devil's Snuffbox *Calvatia gigantea*

Most puffballs are round and white, and rest on the ground without stems. There is a giant among puffballs that is known as the Devil's snuffbox. It may appear suddenly one morning, but it has been growing for two weeks underground. The giant puffball is found all over the world and is excellent to eat while it is still pure white inside. It may weigh up to 20 pounds and be as large as a basketball.

Country boys and girls like to polish their shoes with the small dry puffballs. Press on the puffball and a brown "smoke" pours out through a hole in the top. Look for puffballs in dry pastures and on grassy hillsides.

14

Earthstar *Geastrum triplex*

When you first see an earthstar, you'd never think it is related to a mushroom. Actually, it is a puffball, and both puffballs and mushrooms are fungi. It grows on the ground without a stem and is the color of the earth. It comes up as a small round ball. When it is ripe, the outer skin splits and curves down, often forming five points like a star, but there may be from four to eight points. As the outer skin peels back, it reveals a smaller ball that contains the spores. The points that turn down hold the smaller ball up out of the wetness, and the spores remain dry. When a raindrop hits the spore container, the spores come flying out.

15

Fairy Ring   *Marasmius oreades*

Some summer morning you may see a circle of small reddish tan mushrooms growing on your lawn. You may not have noticed them before but you will probably see them again next year. If the ground is not disturbed they come back in the same place year after year. Each year the circle will be a little larger. Out in the meadows and open fields there are large rings that are believed to be from three to four hundred years old. For many years scientists have been studying this curious ring-growing habit and have not found a satisfactory answer.

Long ago people called mushrooms "children of darkness" because they appeared so suddenly overnight. They thought the rings grew where fairies held their midnight meetings—that as the fairies danced in circles through the night, mushrooms sprang up where their feet touched the ground.

16

Fairy Cups   *Aleuria aurantia*

These brilliant orange cups often decorate the edges of newly graveled roads and logging roads. When they are mature, they are about an inch and a half across. They appear early in the spring and can be found as late as October. When the spores in these cups are ripe, a slight jar will cause hundreds of thousands of spores to shoot into the air. As the wind carries them away, a little cloud of steam seems to be rising from the cups.

People once believed that elves and fairies used these cups to sip the early morning dew.

17

Elves' Saddle   *Helvella lacunosa*

    The elves' saddle is about three inches high, just the right size for a small elf. The cap is black and easily seen in the greenery where it grows. It is found in the fall, and you may see one by itself or a great many close together. The whitish stem is made up of many ribs that are hollow inside. In these hollow ribs lives a tiny insect called a springtail. It seems like a safe place to live but a many-footed animal related to insects, the centipede, often explores the stem of this mushroom to hunt for springtails to eat.

Fly Agaric Mushroom   *Amanita muscaria*

The fly agaric is so colorful, it fairly shouts at you in the woods. Its brilliant red cap is decorated with rough white spots. With its soft, white cottony stem, this is one of nature's most beautiful creations. Look at it and admire it—but leave it where it is. It is a deadly poisonous mushroom. It grows under birch and aspen trees, also in pine and fir forests. It pushes up out of the ground as a small red and white ball. The ball grows larger and larger and finally flattens out into a red cap with white spots. The cap may be six inches wide on a stem five to eight inches tall. Rain will often wash the white spots off the cap, leaving it plain red.

In ancient days, people used this mushroom to kill flies. They would break off small pieces of it and drop them into a saucer of milk. Flies settled on the saucer to drink and soon swelled up and died.

19

Honey Mushroom *Armillaria mellea*

The honey mushroom makes a pretty picture as it grows in large clusters at the base of a living tree. But it is a serious pest on trees. It is a parasite and destroys a tree to get its own food. It sends out roots into the heart of a tree, killing it. It causes great damage in orchards, especially on peach trees. You will see these clusters in late summer on many trees, including oaks, willows, and firs. The honey-colored cap is small, one to four inches across. The clusters aren't always honey-colored. Their tint depends upon the kind of tree they are living on. They have a honey color on a mulberry tree, but on a poplar tree they are cinnamon yellow. They are a yellowish brown on oak trees and reddish brown on fir trees. This interesting mushroom is found all over the world.

20

Inky Cap *Coprinus comatus*

The inky cap is an amazing mushroom that is called an autodigester. When its small, egg-shaped head pushes out of the ground, the cap is wrapped around the stem like a closed umbrella. It grows rapidly and is fully developed within hours. As the cap opens, it turns black and the edges drip an inky fluid that dissolves the cap. In a few hours the cap has disappeared and only a ragged stem is left. Dip a stick into the black "ink" and you will find that you can write with it. The inky cap grows in clusters in cool, wet weather. It appears in the spring and again in the fall. Look for it around farm buildings, city dumps and in gravel by the side of the road.

21

Milk Cap   *Lactarius deliciosus*

For those people who dare to pick wild mushrooms, the milk cap is delicious when baked in a covered dish with bacon or butter; however, its vivid carrot color stained with green may not be appealing to the appetite. When one is cut or bruised, it drips a thick milky juice which is also carrot color. In a few minutes the bruised place turns a coppery green. As the cap grows older, the carrot tint fades and the entire mushroom turns coppery green.

22

Morel   *Morchella esculenta*

Everyone seems to agree that the morel has the best flavor of all mushrooms. And it can't be mistaken for another kind. It is a spring mushroom growing in grassy fields or under deciduous trees. It is small, not more than four inches high, and it grows all over North America and Europe. The brown cap is full of holes and looks wrinkled—you might compare it with a sponge. Put your nose down and sniff. It has a pleasant odor.

There is an interesting old folk tale from Germany. The devil was in a bad temper one day when he met an old wrinkled woman who was in his way. He seized her and cut her up into small pieces. As he walked on he tossed the pieces around over the ground. Everywhere a piece fell, a morel grew. In that area, an old woman with a wrinkled face is called a "morchel."

23

Old Man of the Woods   *Strobilomyces floccopus*

The "old man" is a sturdy little mushroom dressed in gray and black. Both the cap and the stem are covered with blackish brown scales. These mushrooms usually stand alone but sometimes keep company in twos and threes. In late summer you will find them standing on the edges of small pools in the woods. They may be growing on the ground or attached to rotten wood.

24

Parasol Mushroom   *Macrolepiota procera*

The parasol mushroom is beautifully marked with thick brown scales on the cap and stem. It stands about eight inches high, and the cap may be an equal eight inches across. It's a common mushroom found in meadows and open woods all summer. It may appear in your gardens and pastures too.

In stories and poetry for children, the parasol mushroom is used by elves and tiny creatures of the woods. They keep dry with it when it rains or take a nap under its shade when the sun is hot. Even today as you bend over to examine it, a small mouse may scurry away from under it or a solemn toad may stare out at you and refuse to move.

25

Squirrel's Bread *Boletus edulis*

Squirrel's bread is a hardy mushroom with a brown, crusty cap. It looks like a warm muffin fresh out of the oven. The underside of the cap is yellow and it has a short, fat stem. These mushrooms have a sweet, nutty flavor that attracts squirrels, which carry them off to their nests for later feeding. Human mushroom-eaters like to use them in gravy or stew. You will find them growing on the ground in open places from June to October. They are common all over North America and Europe.

26

Thimble Mushroom   *Verpa bohemica*

This is a long, thin mushroom wearing a brown cap. It looks like a finger wearing a thimble. The creamy white stem is about five inches long, and the thimble-shaped cap is folded into wrinkles. Look for it along riverbanks and in open woods where there are maple and cottonwood trees. It comes up early in the spring before the leaves are out on the trees.

27

Witches' Butter   *Dacrymyces palmatus*

This is a curious quivering fungus found on logs and stumps, and on twigs on the ground. It looks like blobs of brightly colored butter and so is often called "witches' butter." It isn't smooth, however, but a small wrinkled, twisted mass. Though this is less than two inches across, it is quite conspicuous during wet weather. When it becomes dry it shrivels to a dull, hard lump. It is too small and too tasteless to be worth eating, but it does add a sparkle to the woods with its unexpected bright color.

28

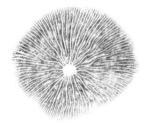

Making Spore Prints

When a scientist is trying to identify a mushroom that is new to him, it is necessary to know the color of the spores. They may be white, brown, yellow, black, or pink. He finds the color by making a spore print. To make this, he cuts the stem from his mushroom and places the cap flat on a piece of white paper. In an hour or two there should be enough spores on the paper to show the color.

You might like to make a spore print to frame and keep. Choose a fresh mushroom with a flat cap. Cut off the stem and place the cap flat on a sheet of paper. Cover the cap with a jar so no breath of air will disturb the falling spores and spoil your pattern. Leave it for three or four hours. Remove the jar and cap very carefully and spray the print with a clear lacquer or fixative. You will find this in hobby shops and other stores. Spray it from a distance so the spraying doesn't disturb the spores.

It's interesting to experiment with colored sheets of paper. For instance, you can make a white print on red, a brown print on yellow, or a black print on light green.

29

Index

Glossary

autodigester: a plant that digests or dissolves itself

cap: the umbrella-like top of the mushroom

centipede: a small animal related to insects, with a long flattened body divided into many parts, with one pair of legs to each part

conifer: an evergreen tree that usually has cones, such as pine and fir

deciduous: referring to trees that drop their leaves in the fall

edible: fit to be eaten

eggs: common name of the small spore sacs in the "nest" of the "bird's nest" mushroom

fungus: a spore-bearing plant that does not make its own food

gills: thin plates of tissue on the underside of a mushroom cap

identify: to know a fungus so well that you can name it

mushroom: the spore-producing body of some fungi, both edible and poisonous species

mycelium: the underground threads that make up the plant part of an individual fungus

parasite: a plant living on another plant to the injury of the second one (or an animal living in a similar way)

species: a class of plants having certain traits in common

spores: the reproductive cells of fungi

springtail: a tiny wingless insect about the size of a flea

toadstool: a common name frequently used for mushroom

tubes: very small holes in the tissue on the underside of the mushroom cap